Fantasy Art

mini adult coloring book

by

Tabz Jones

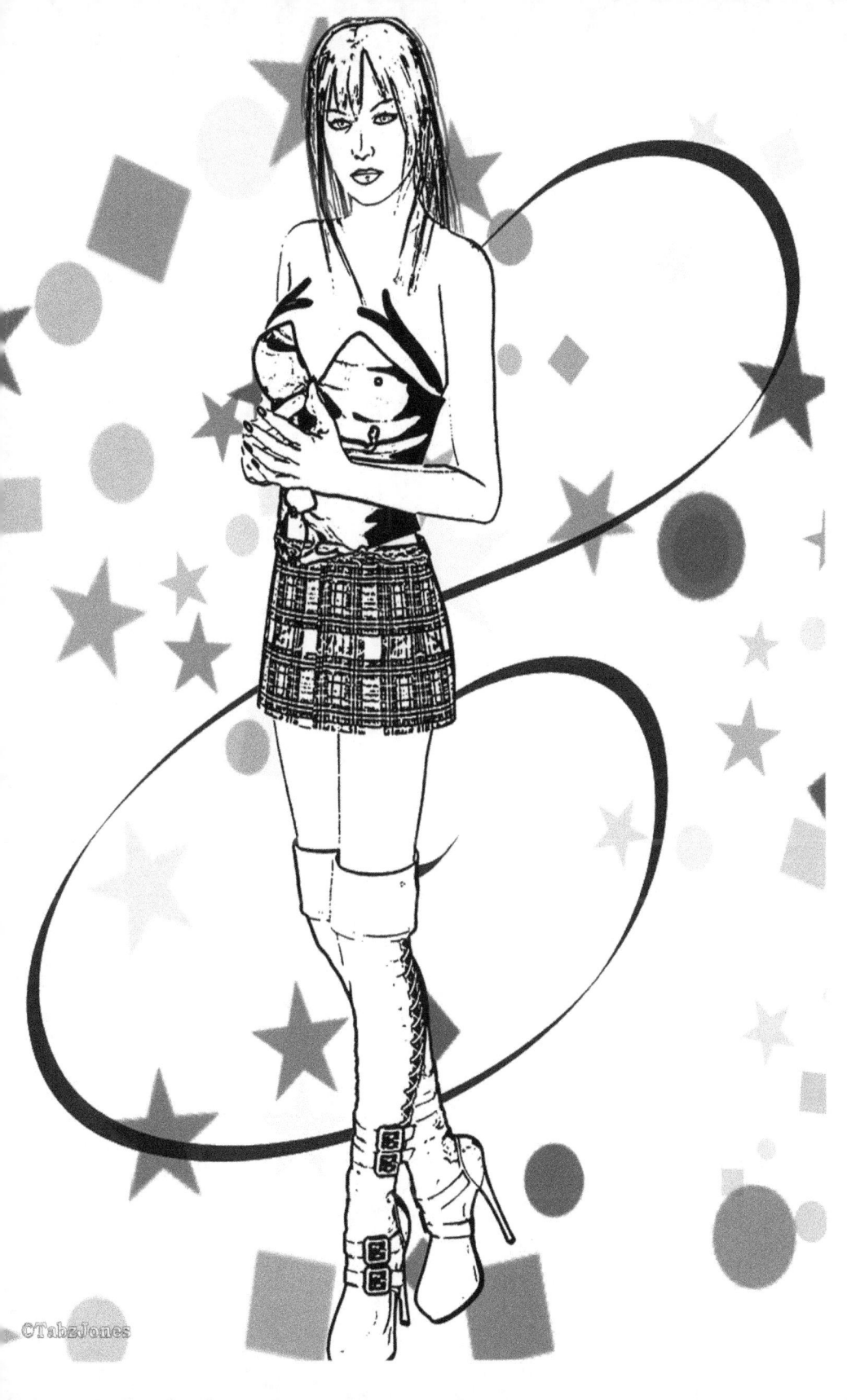

©TabzJones

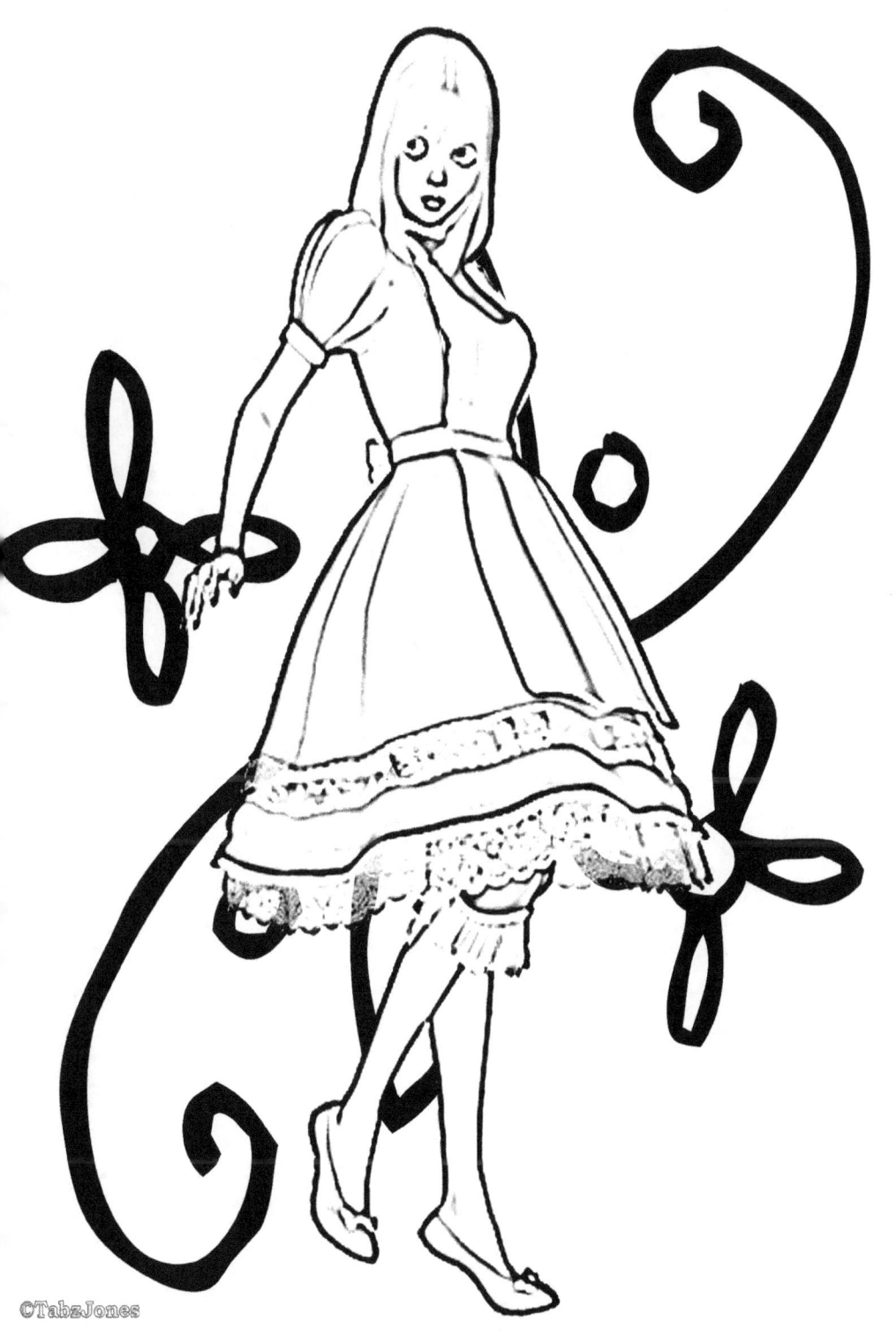

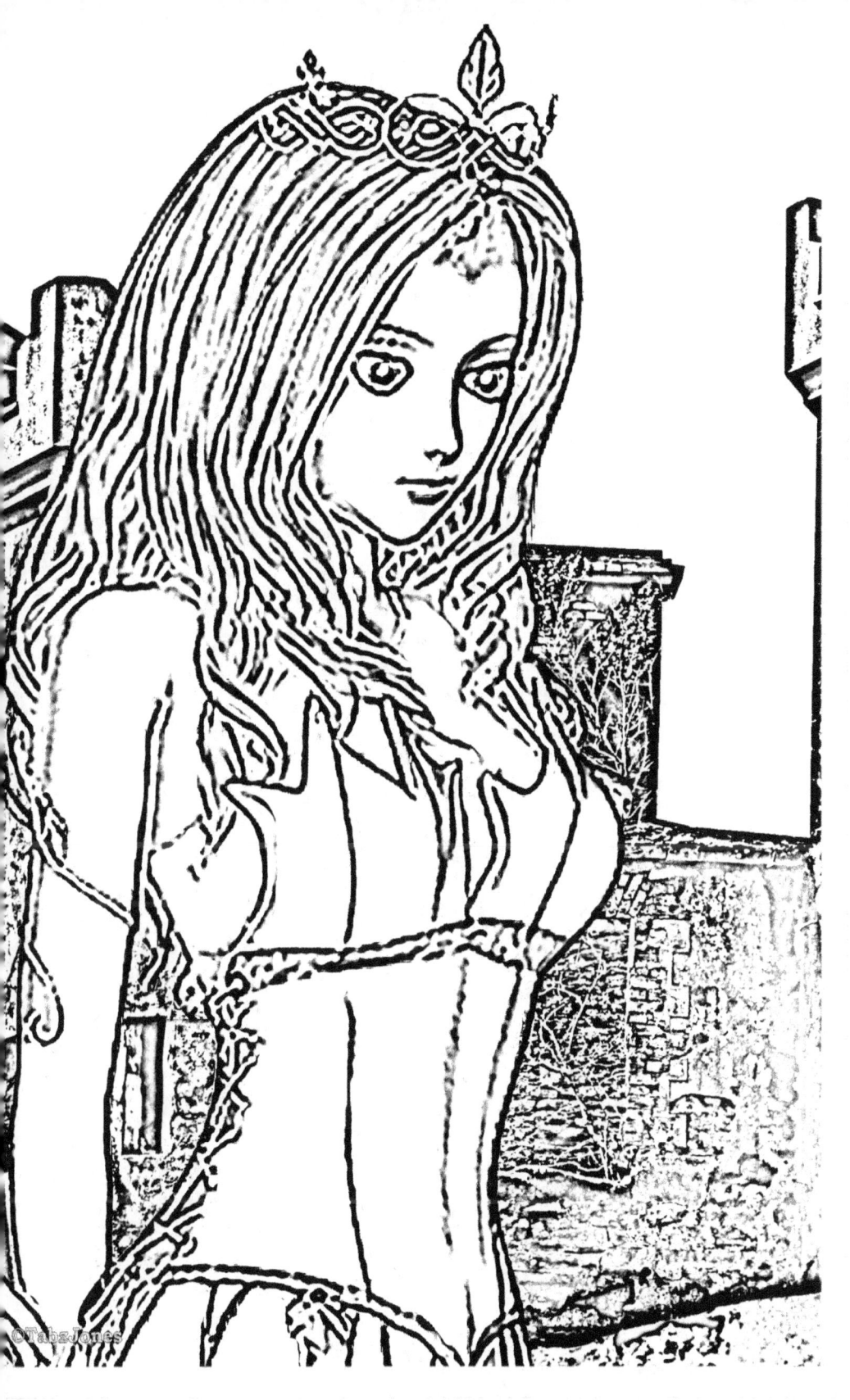

©TabzJones

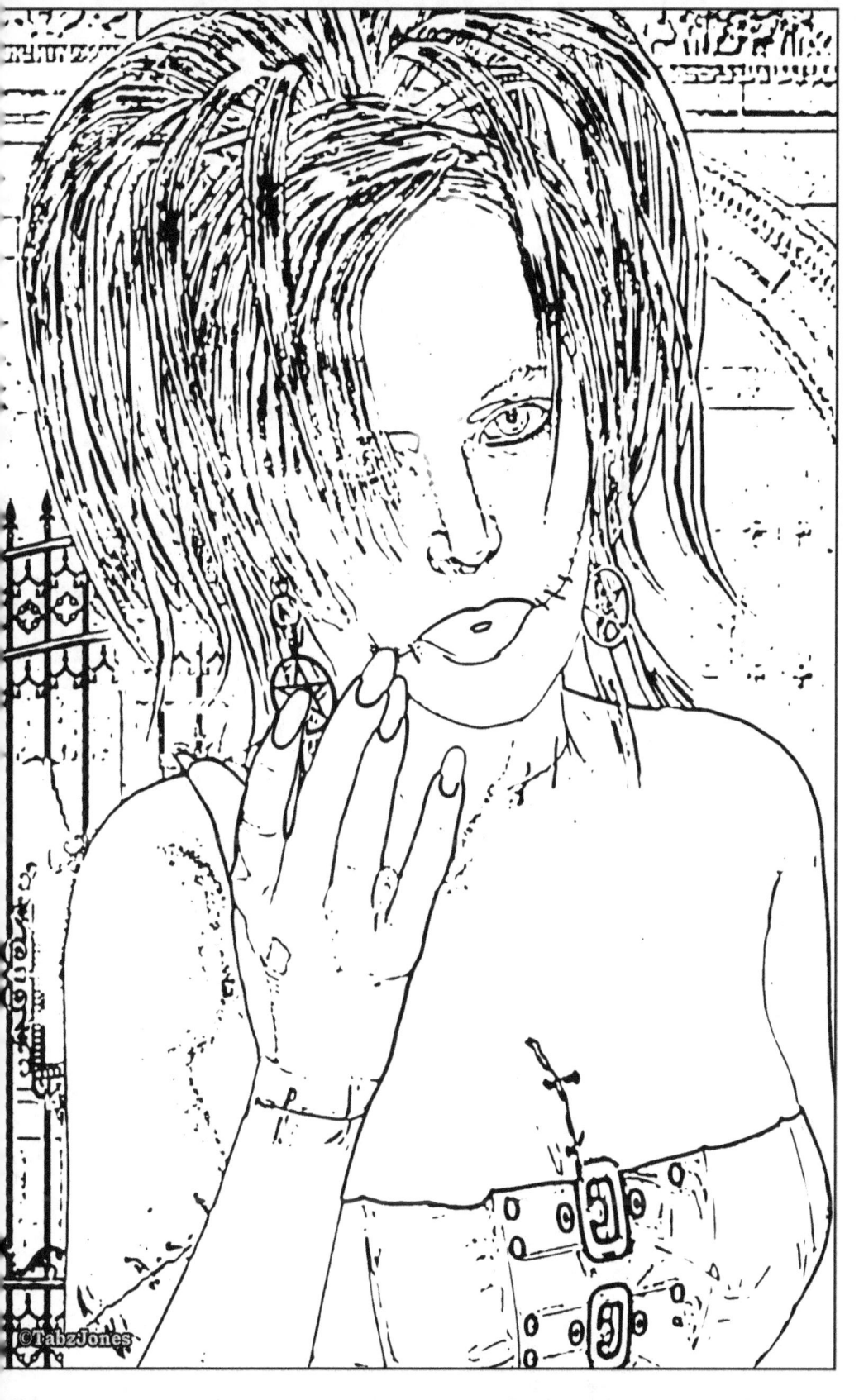

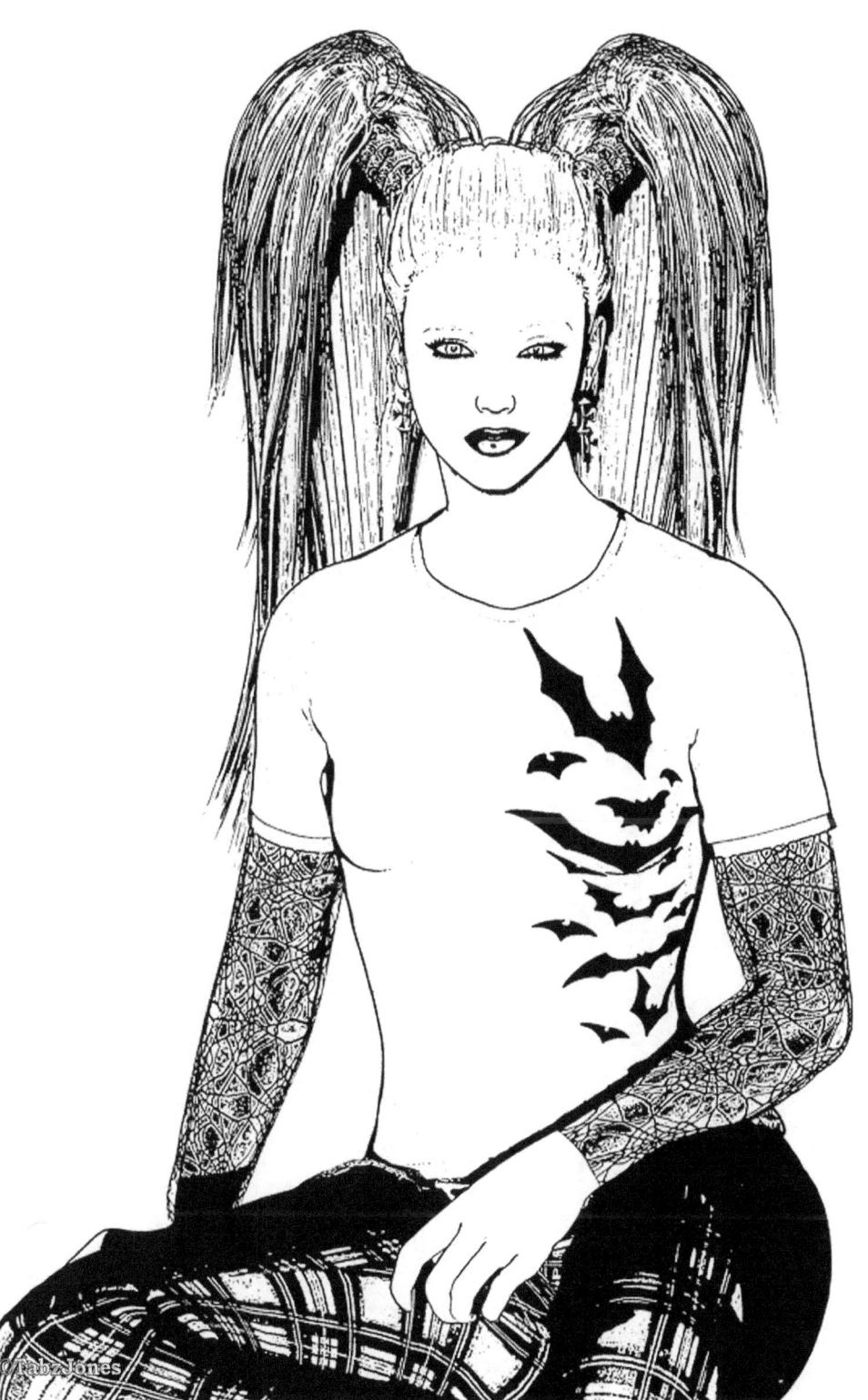

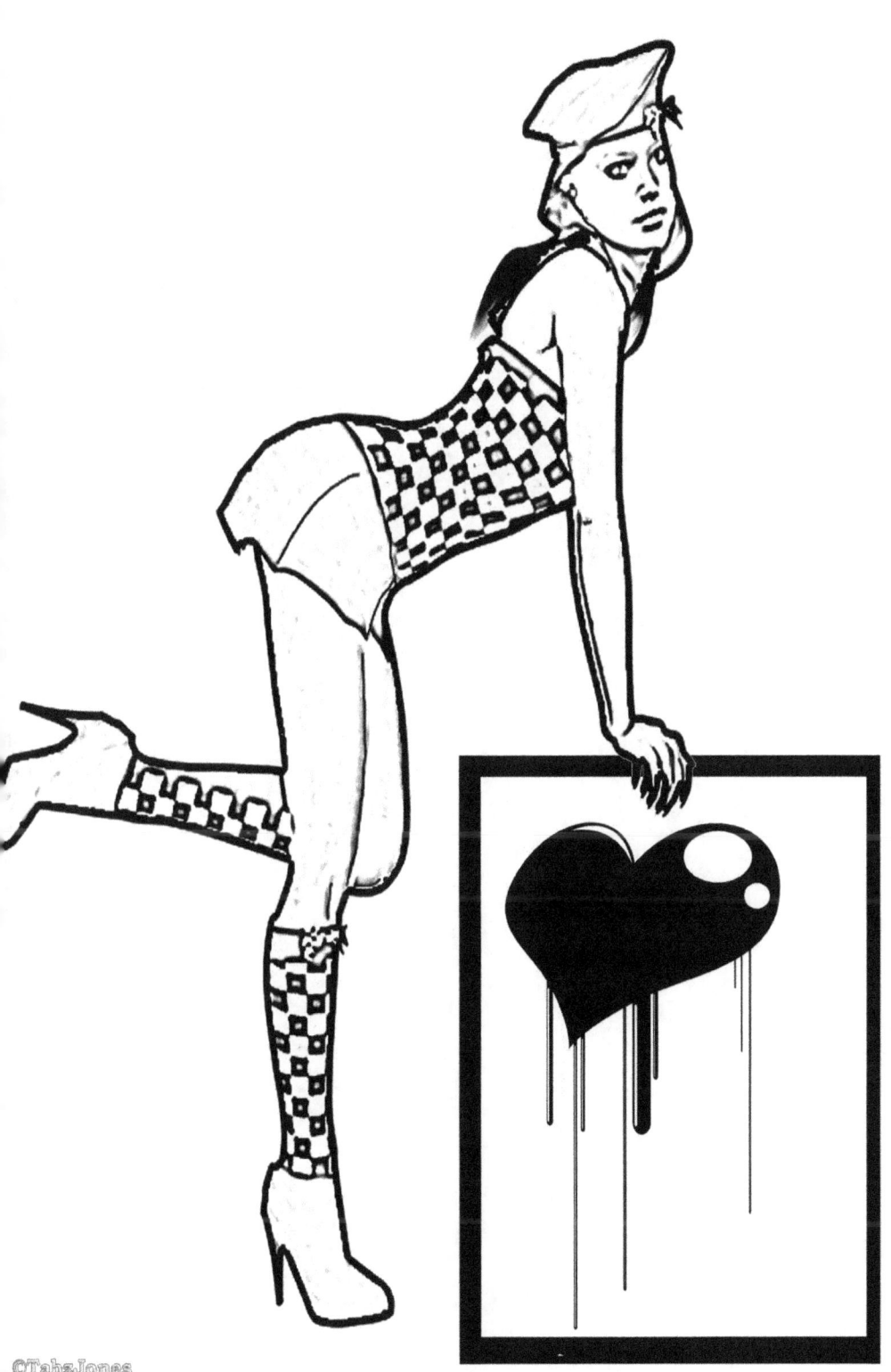

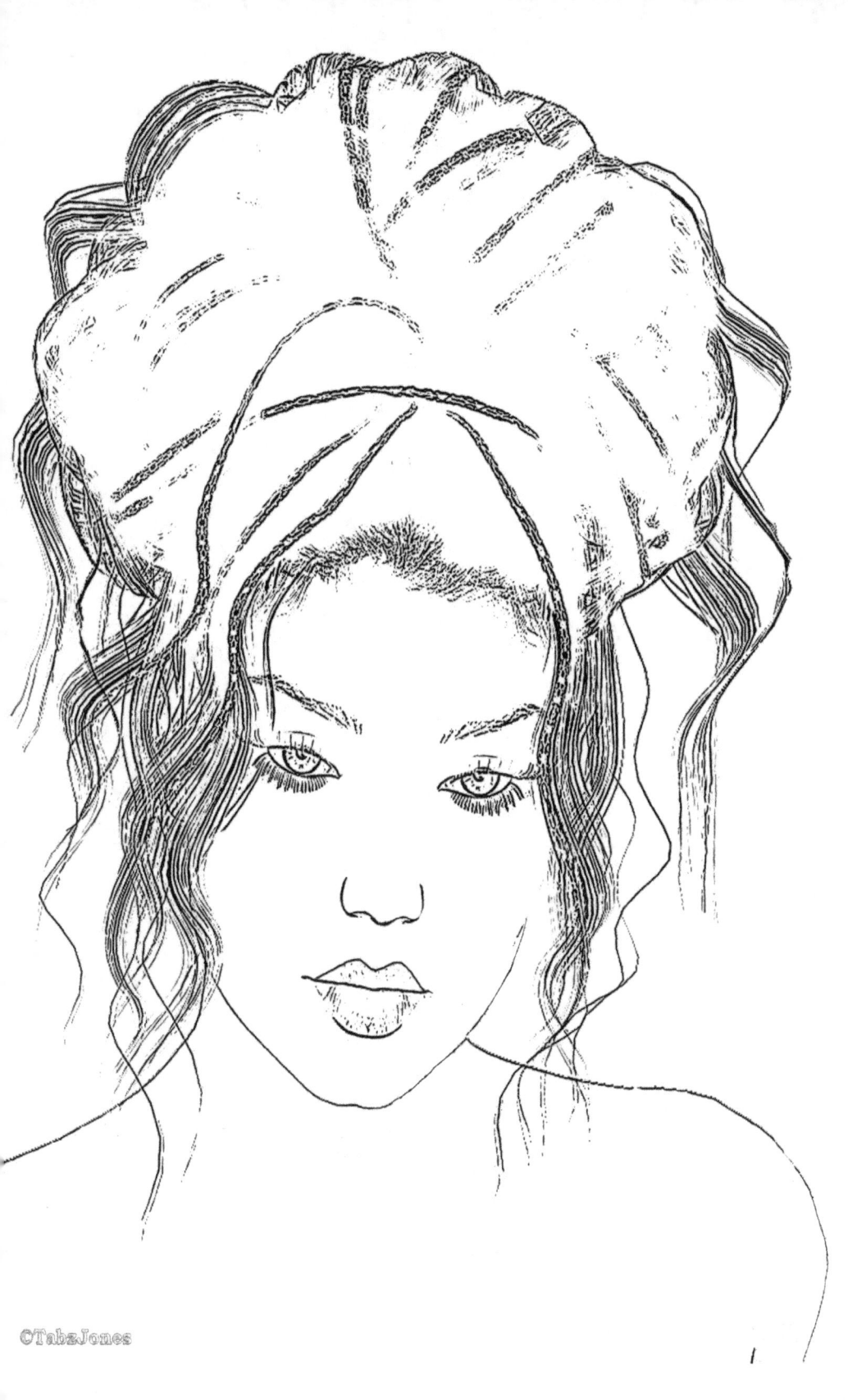

©TabaJones

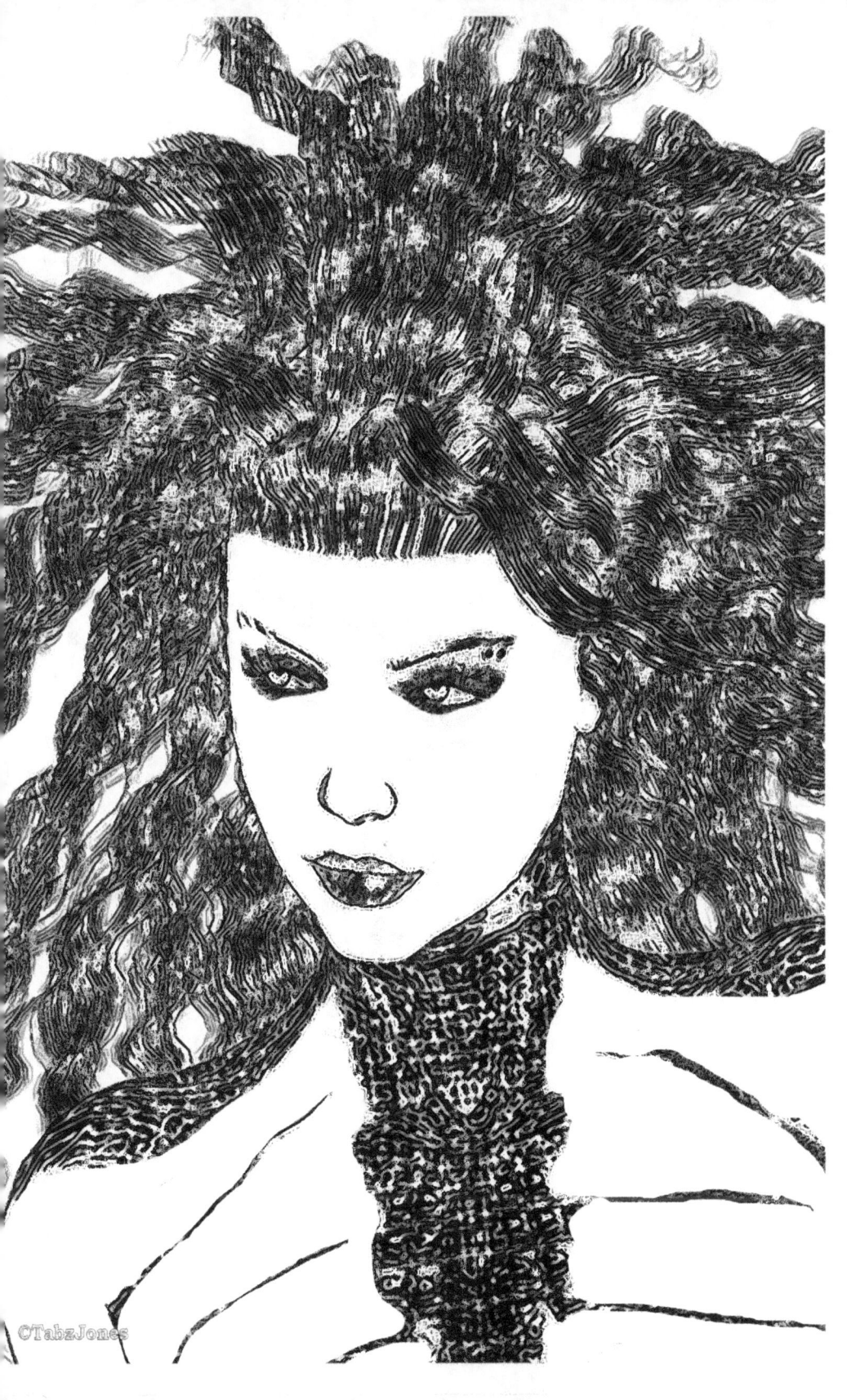

©TabzJones

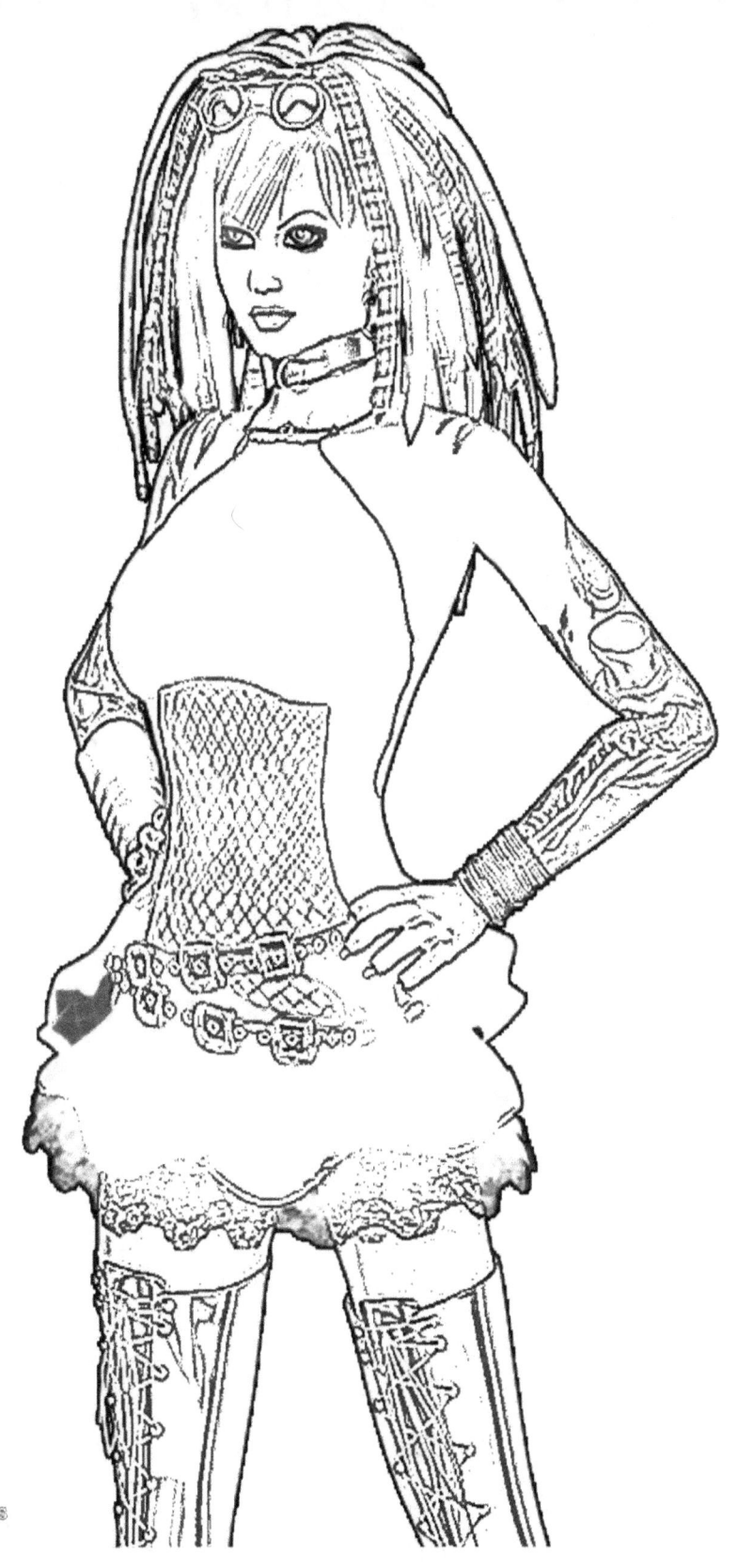

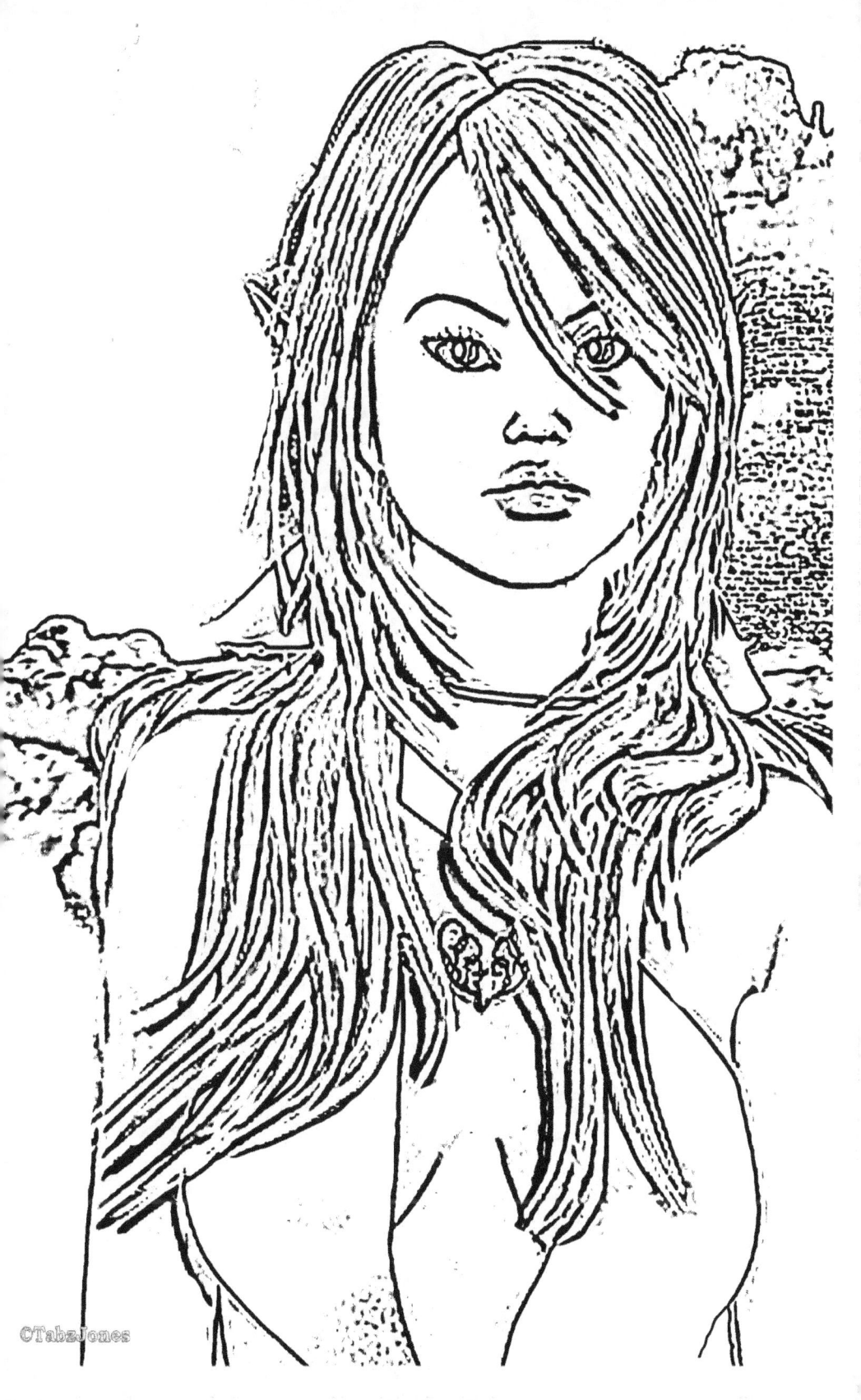

©TabaJones

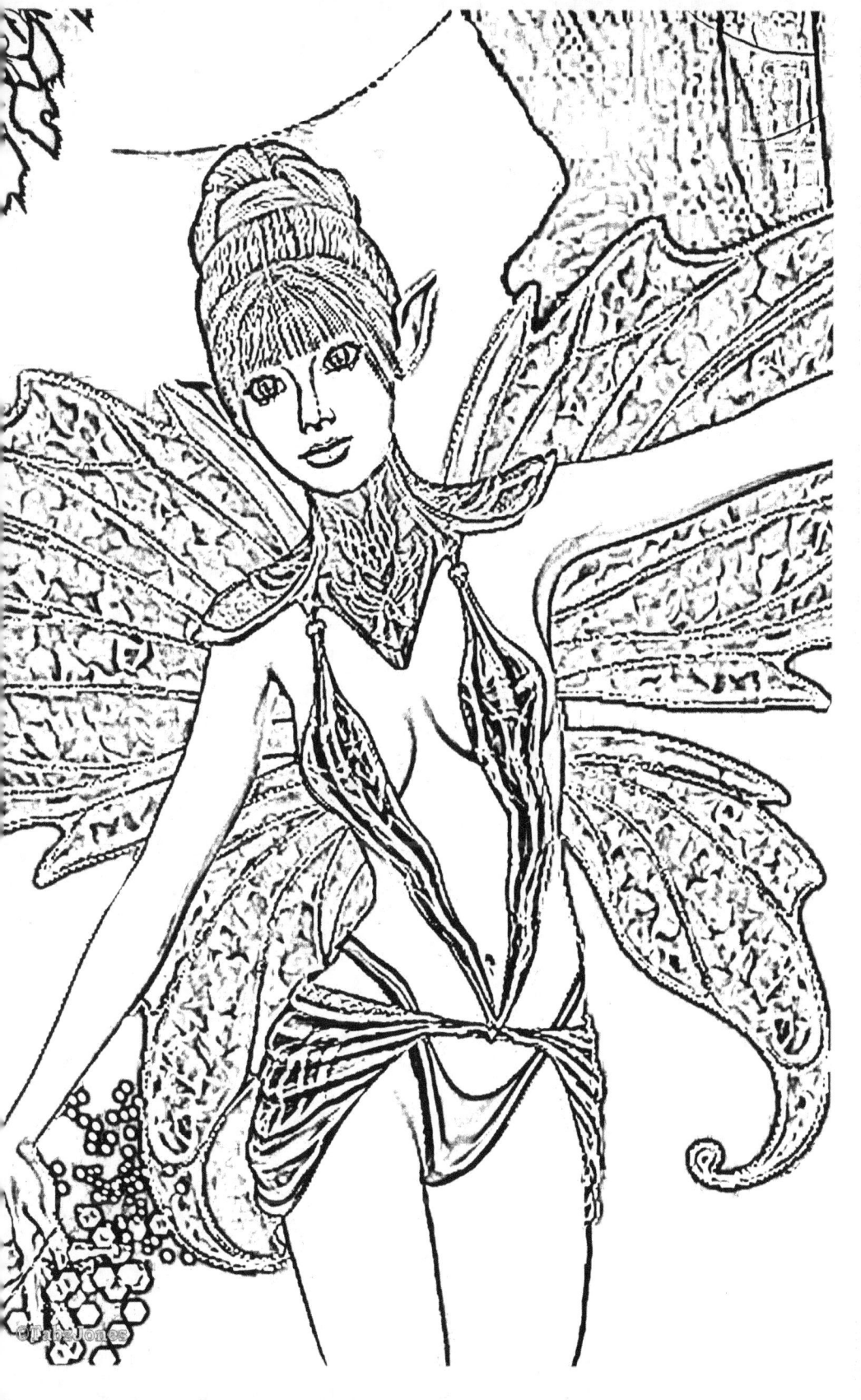

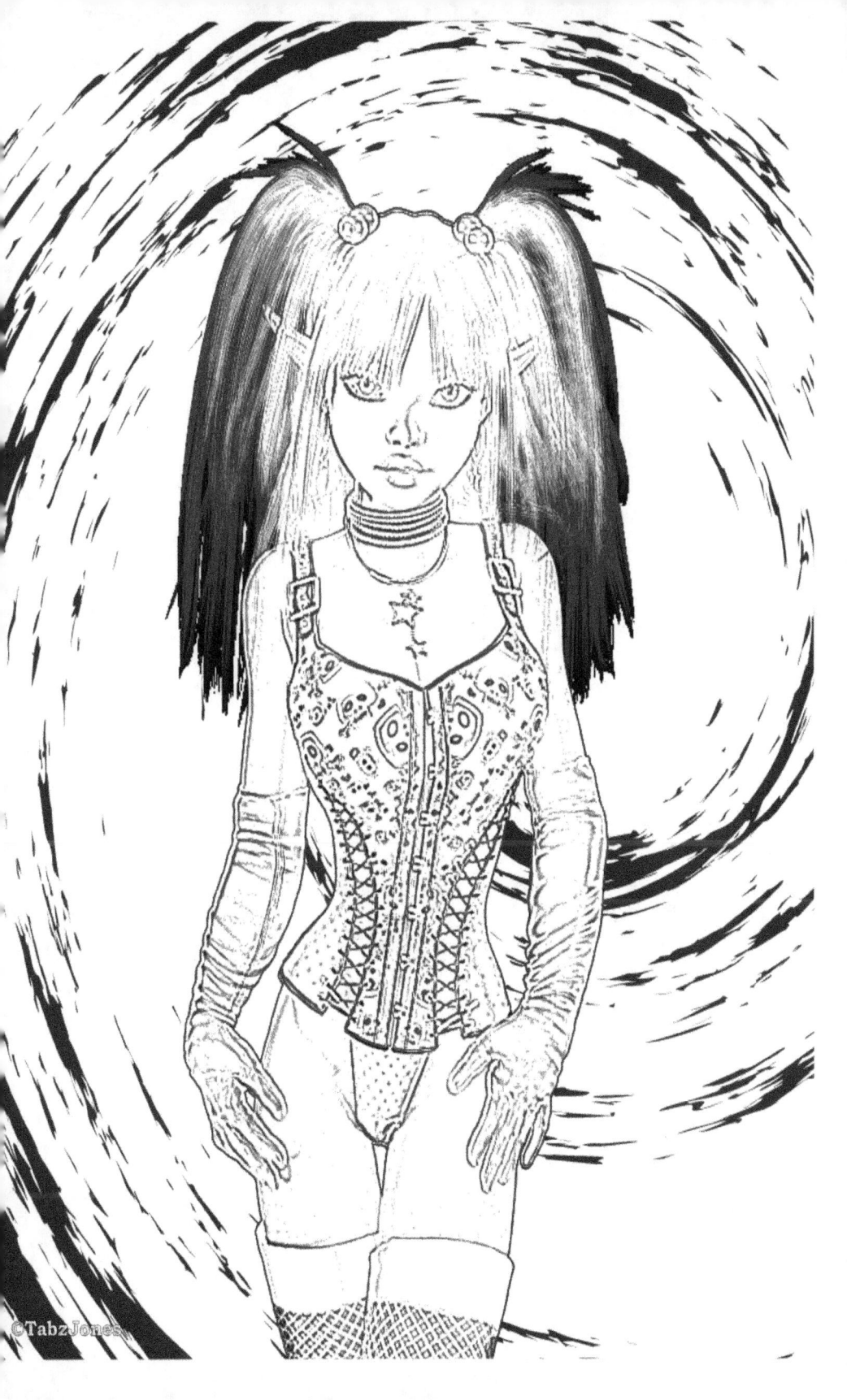

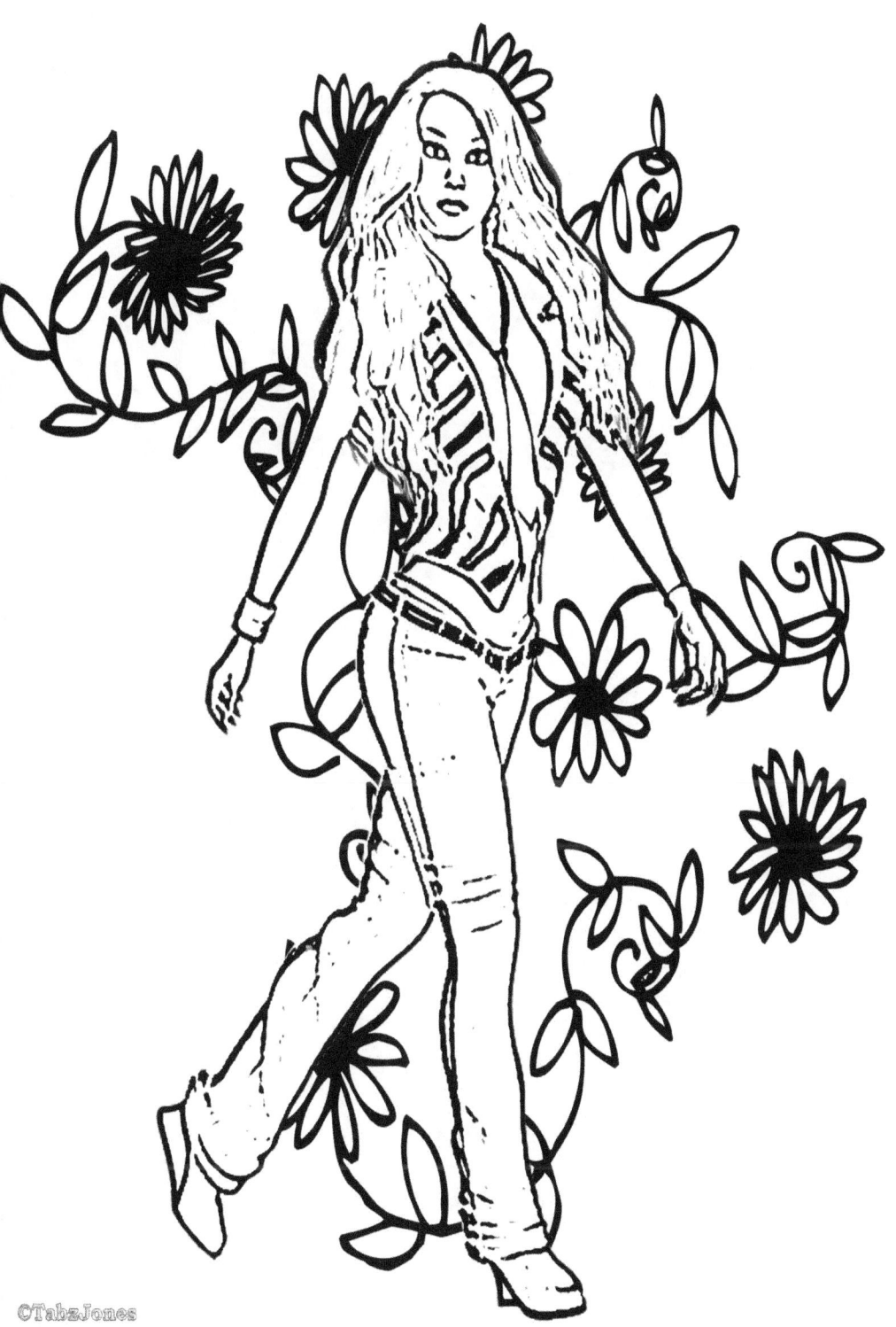

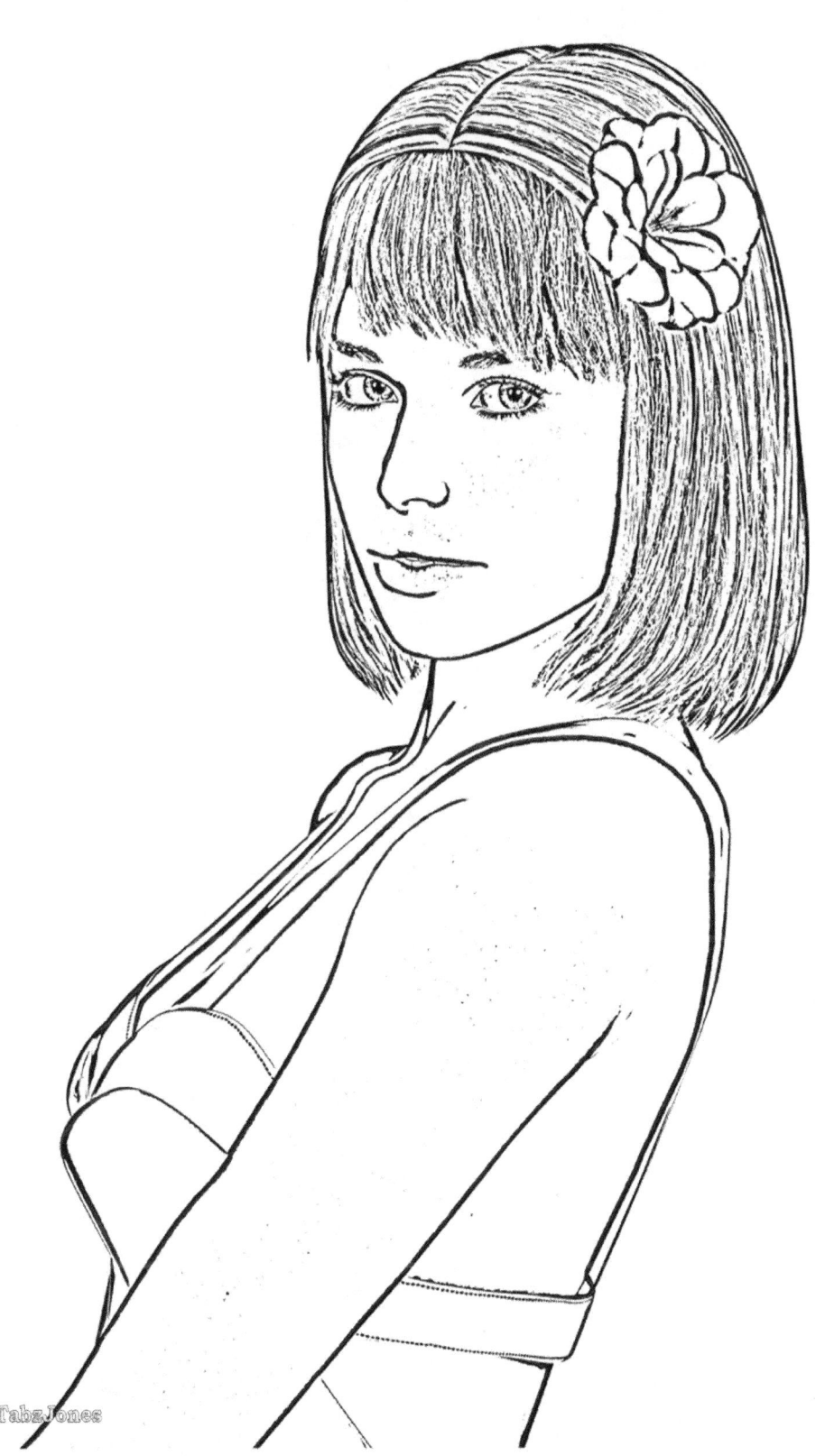

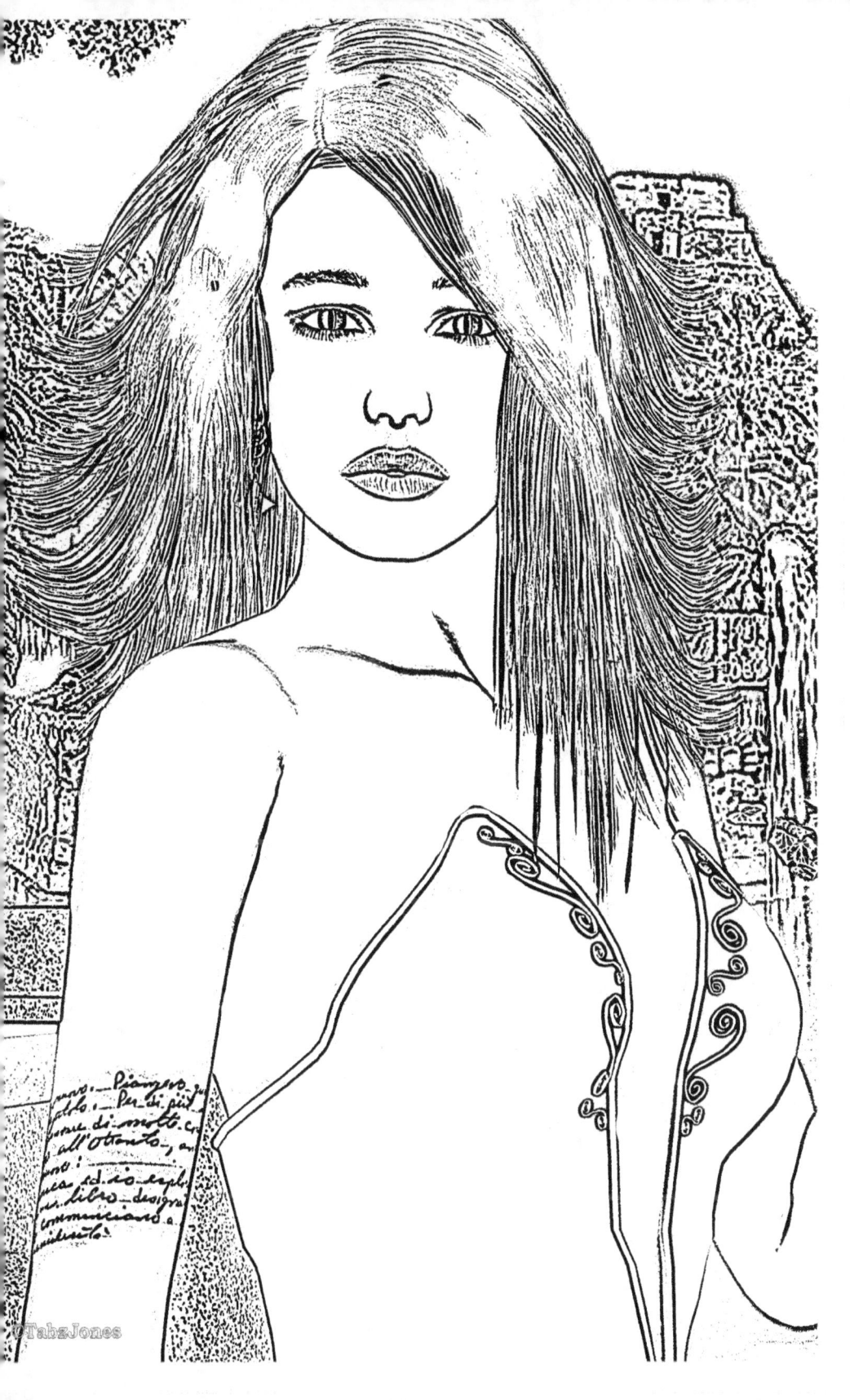

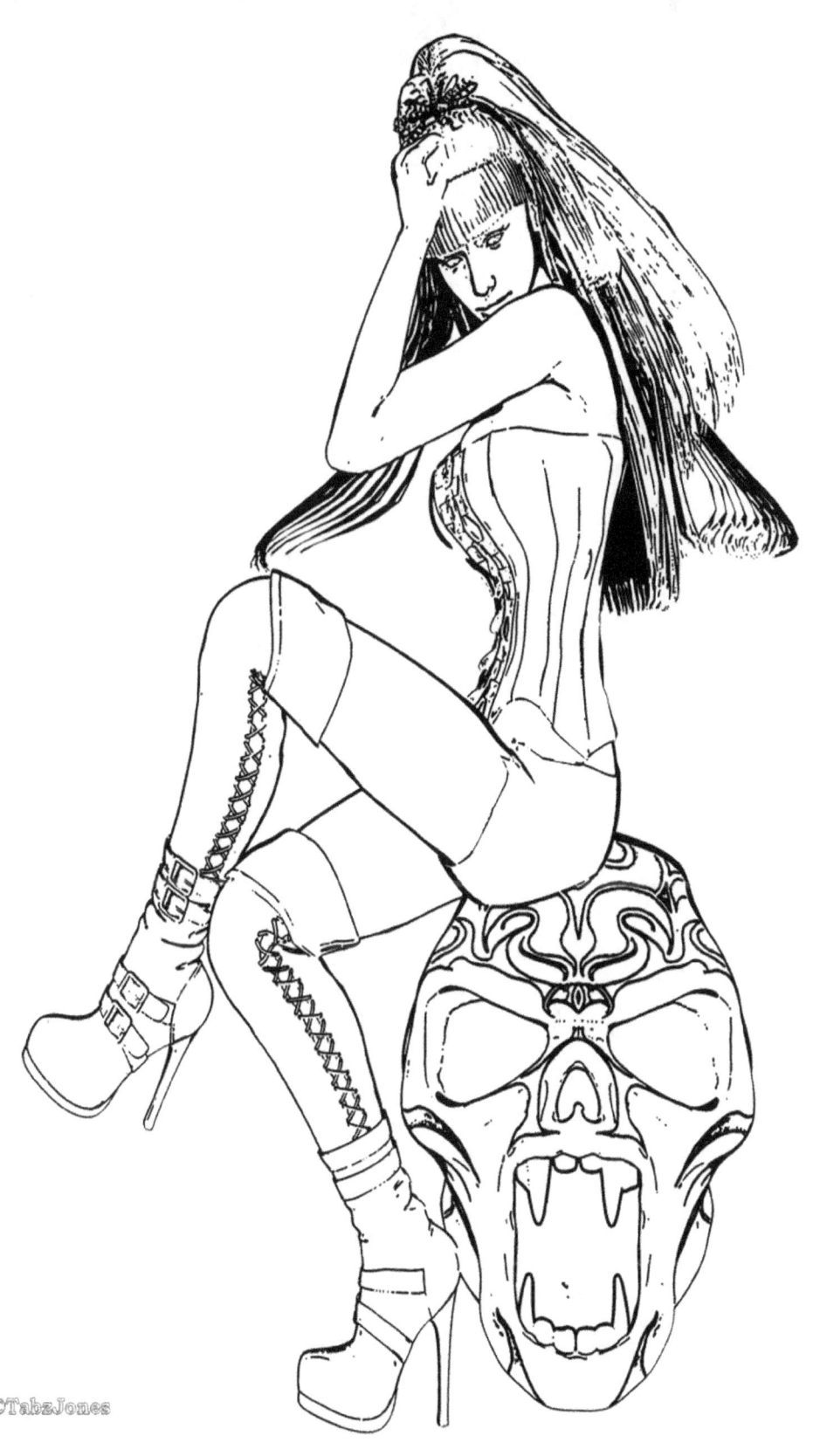

©TabzJones

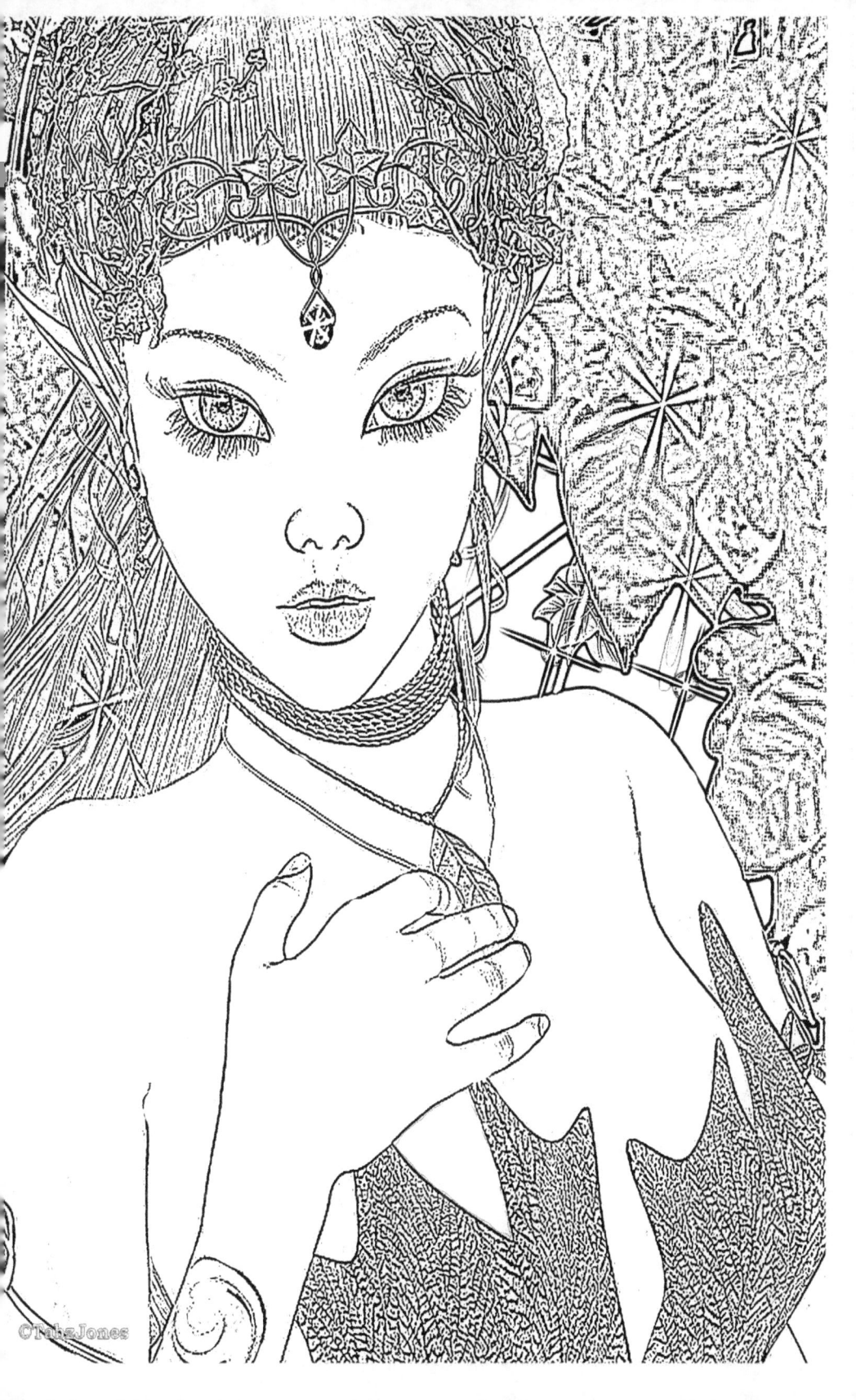

©TalaJones

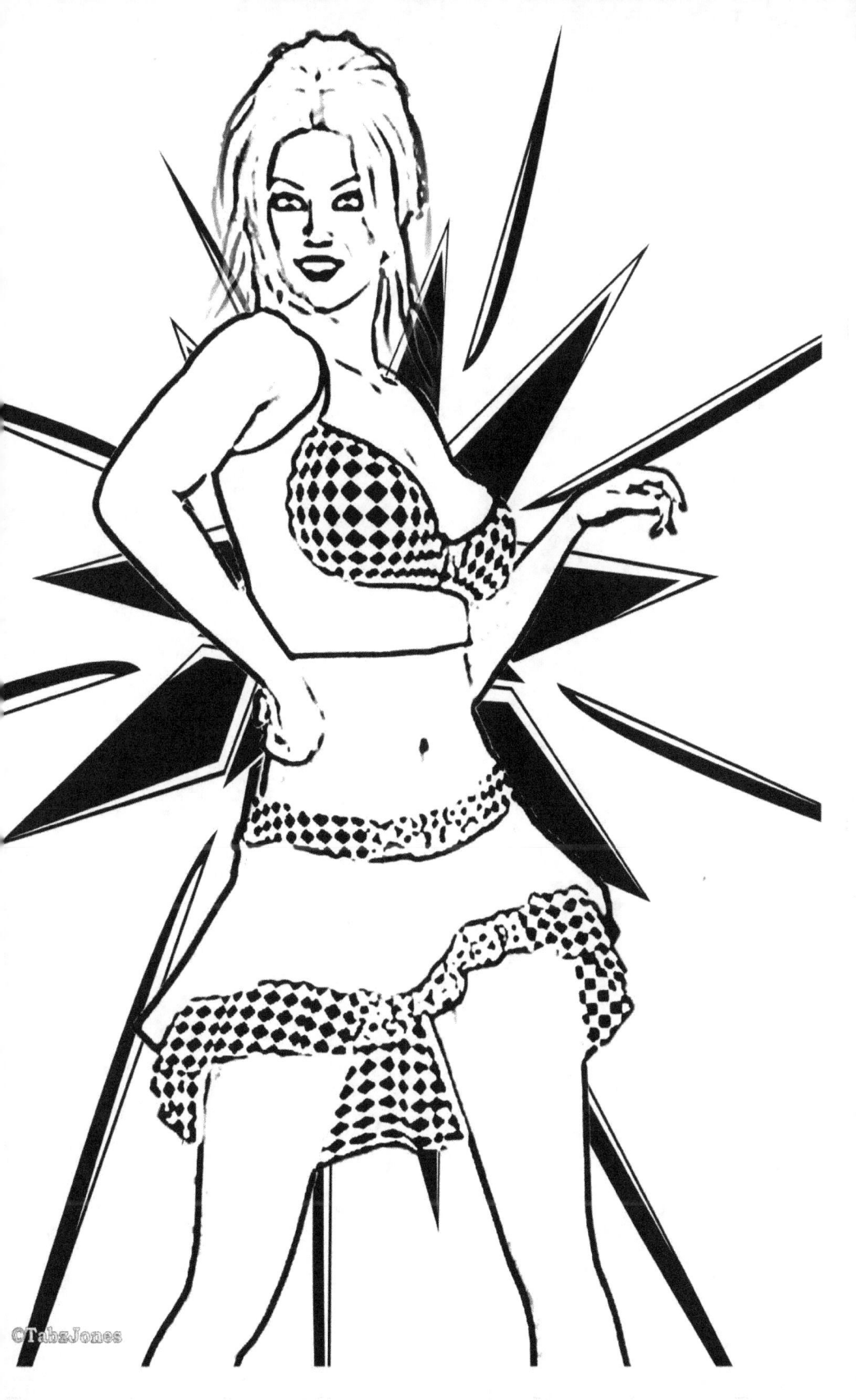

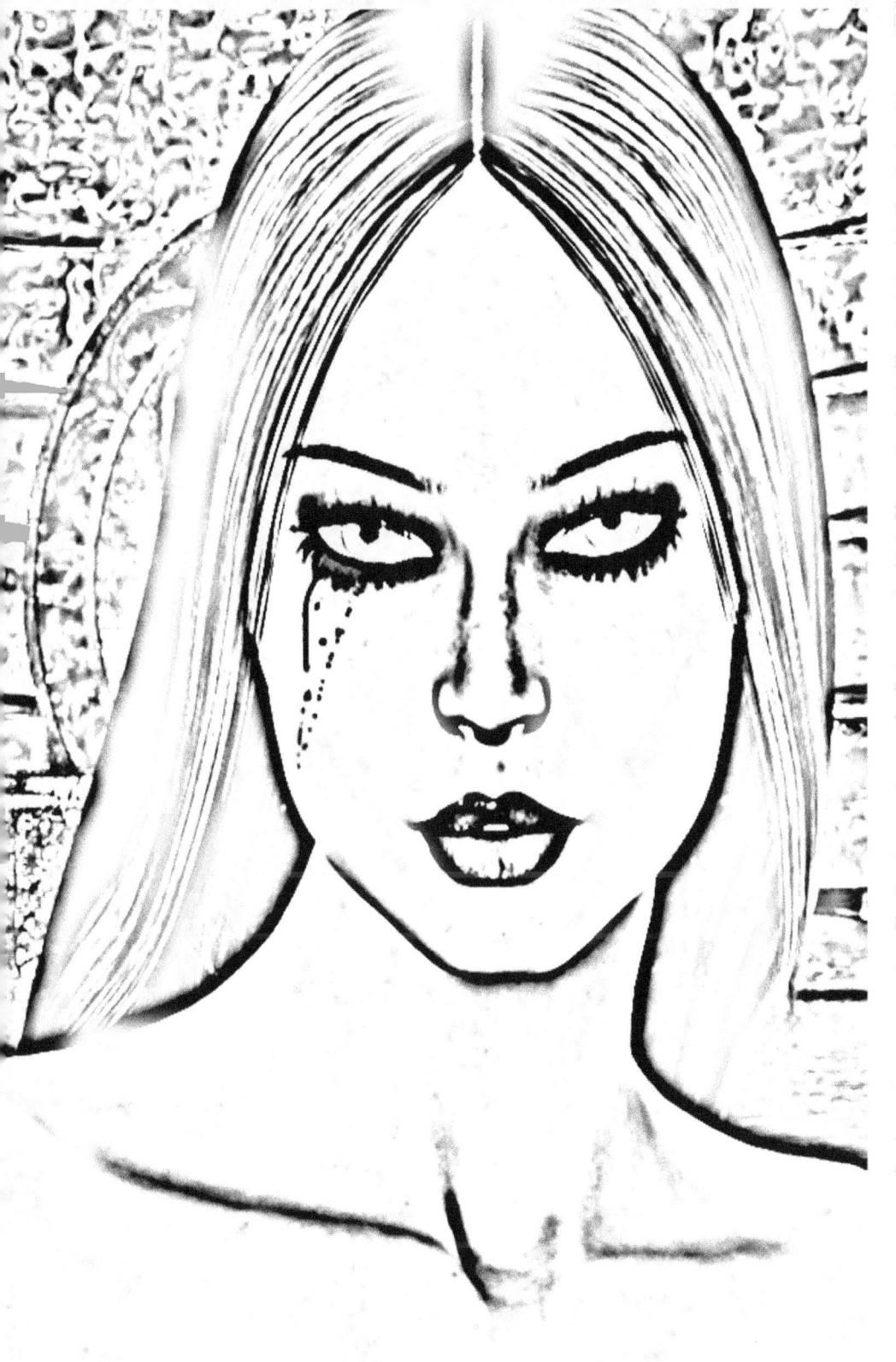

©TabzJones

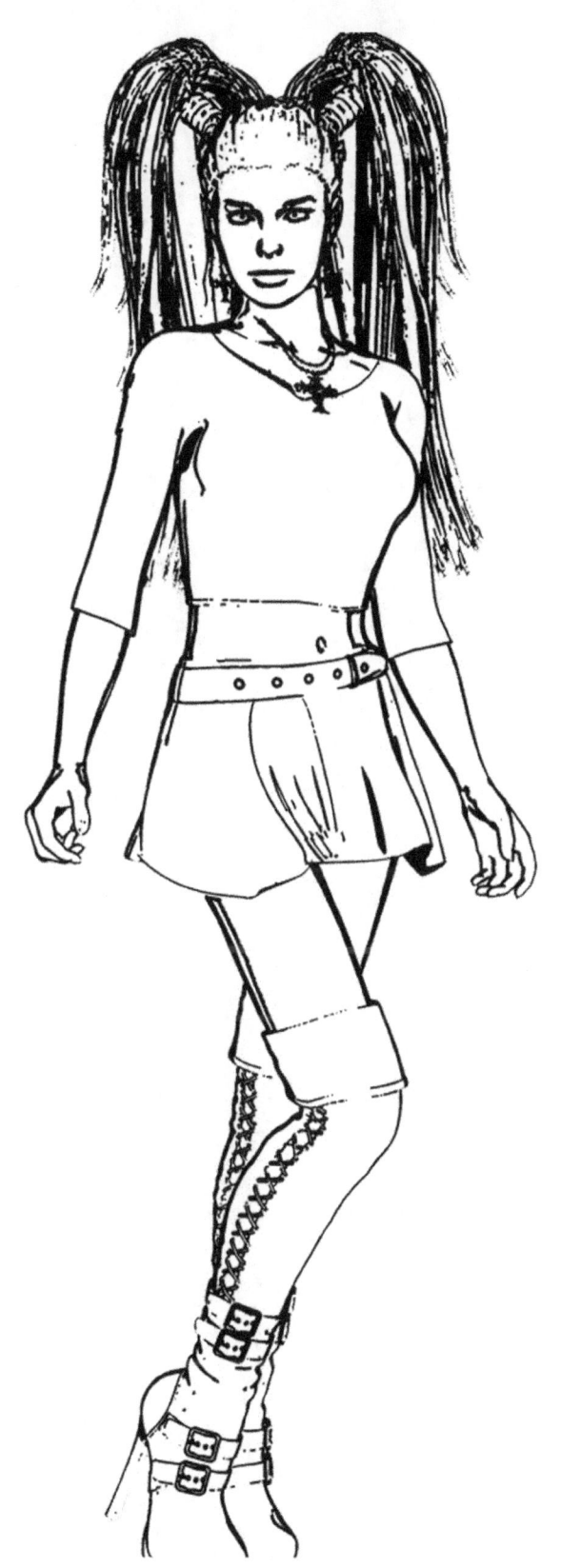

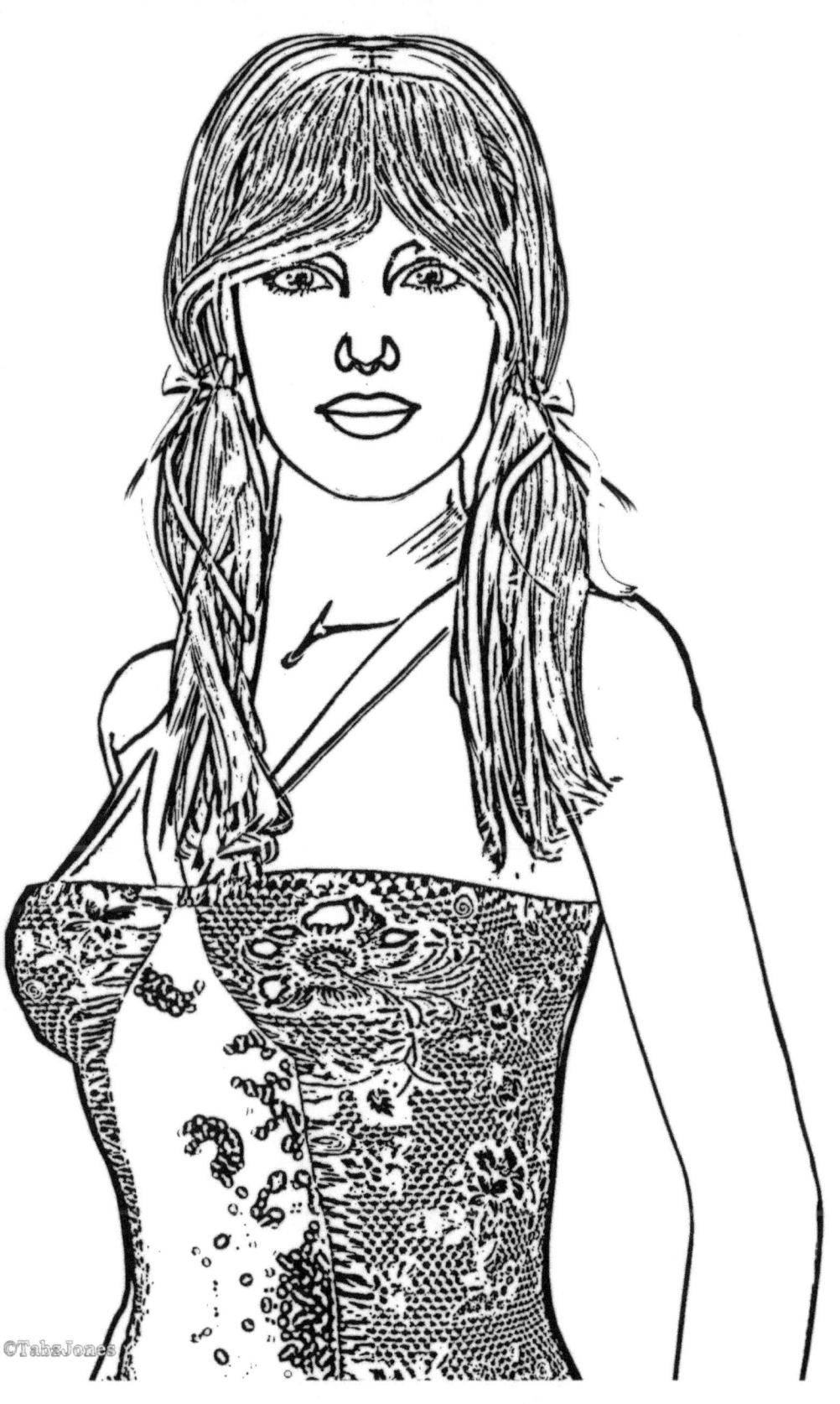

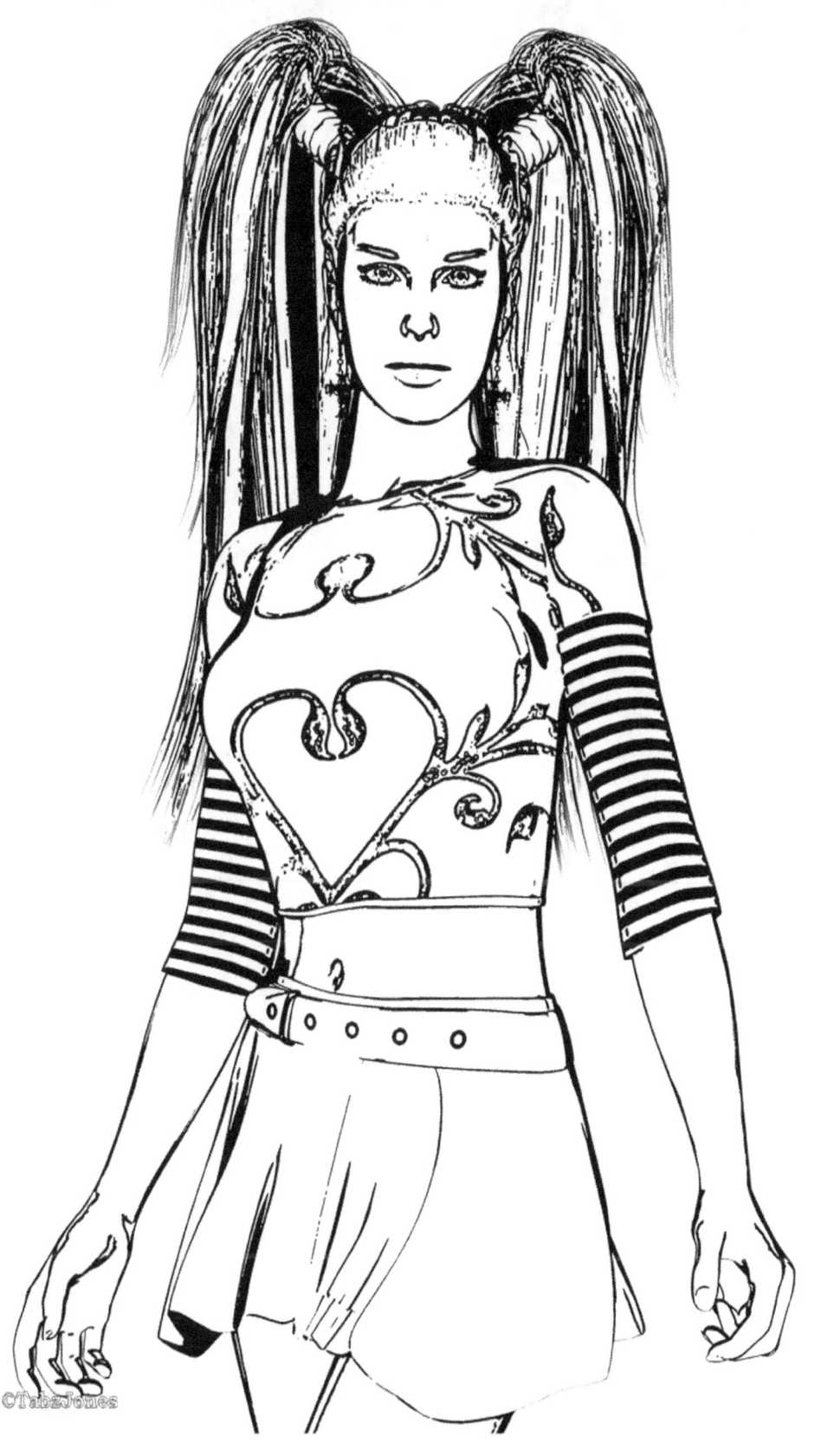
©TabzJones

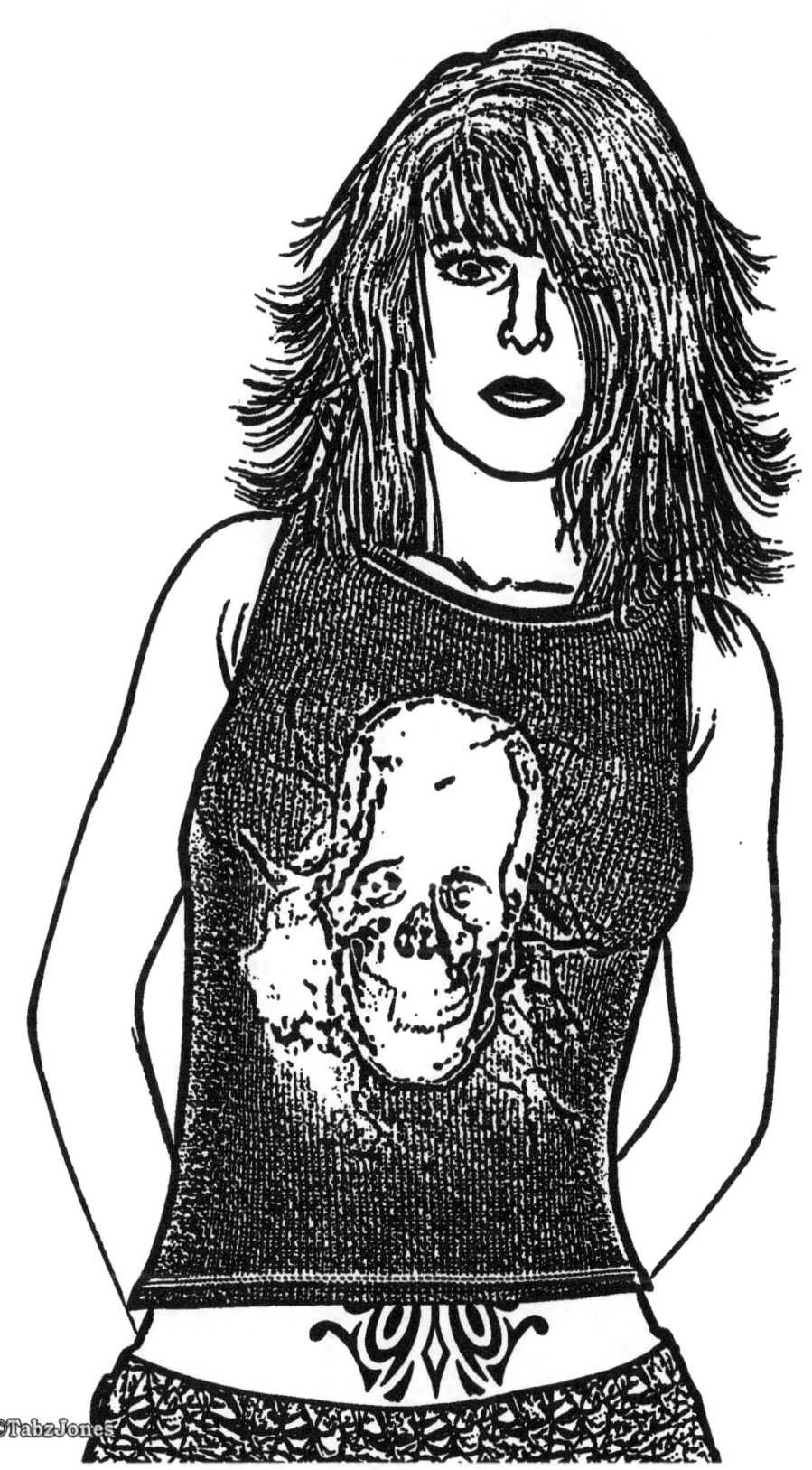

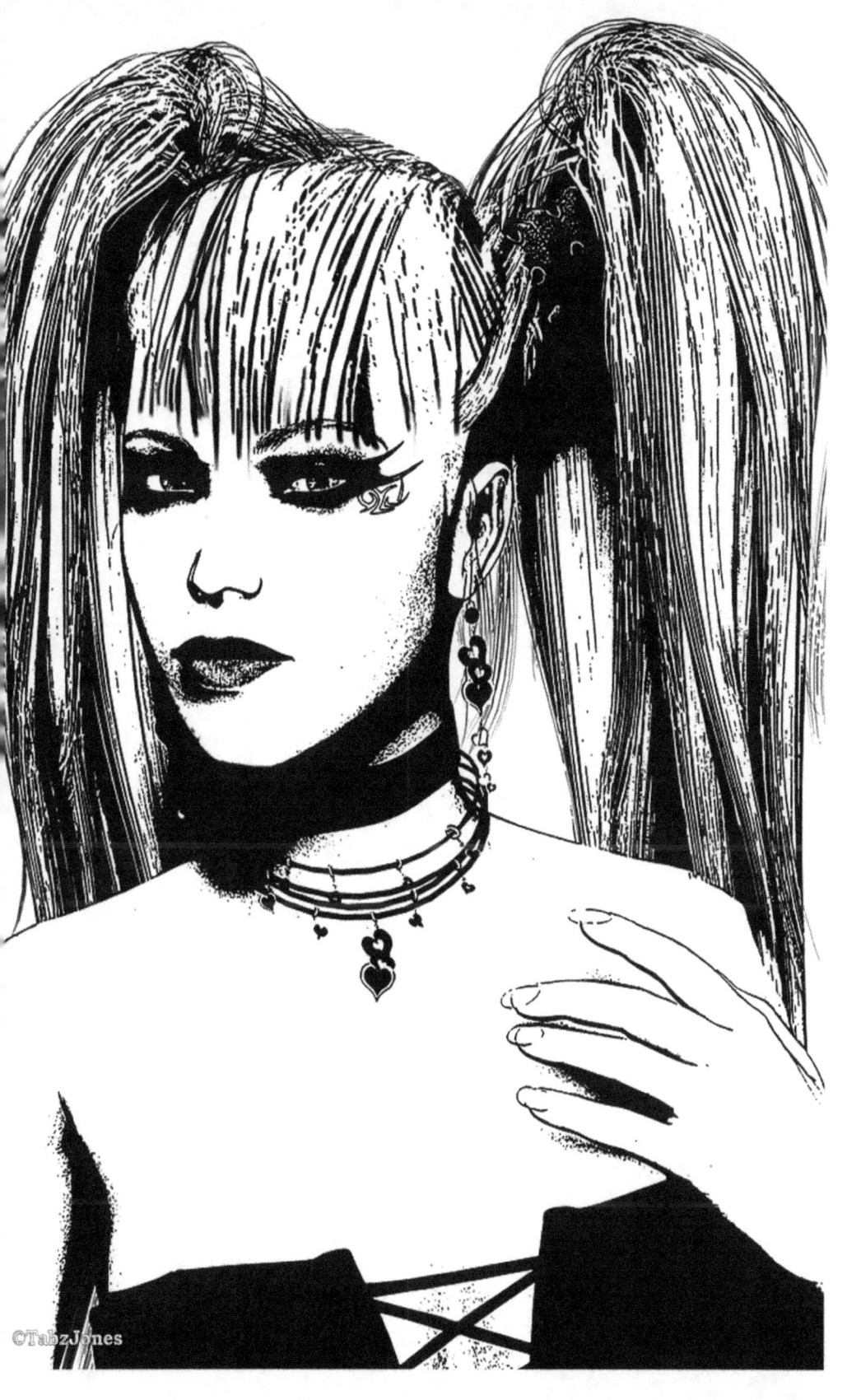

©TabzJones

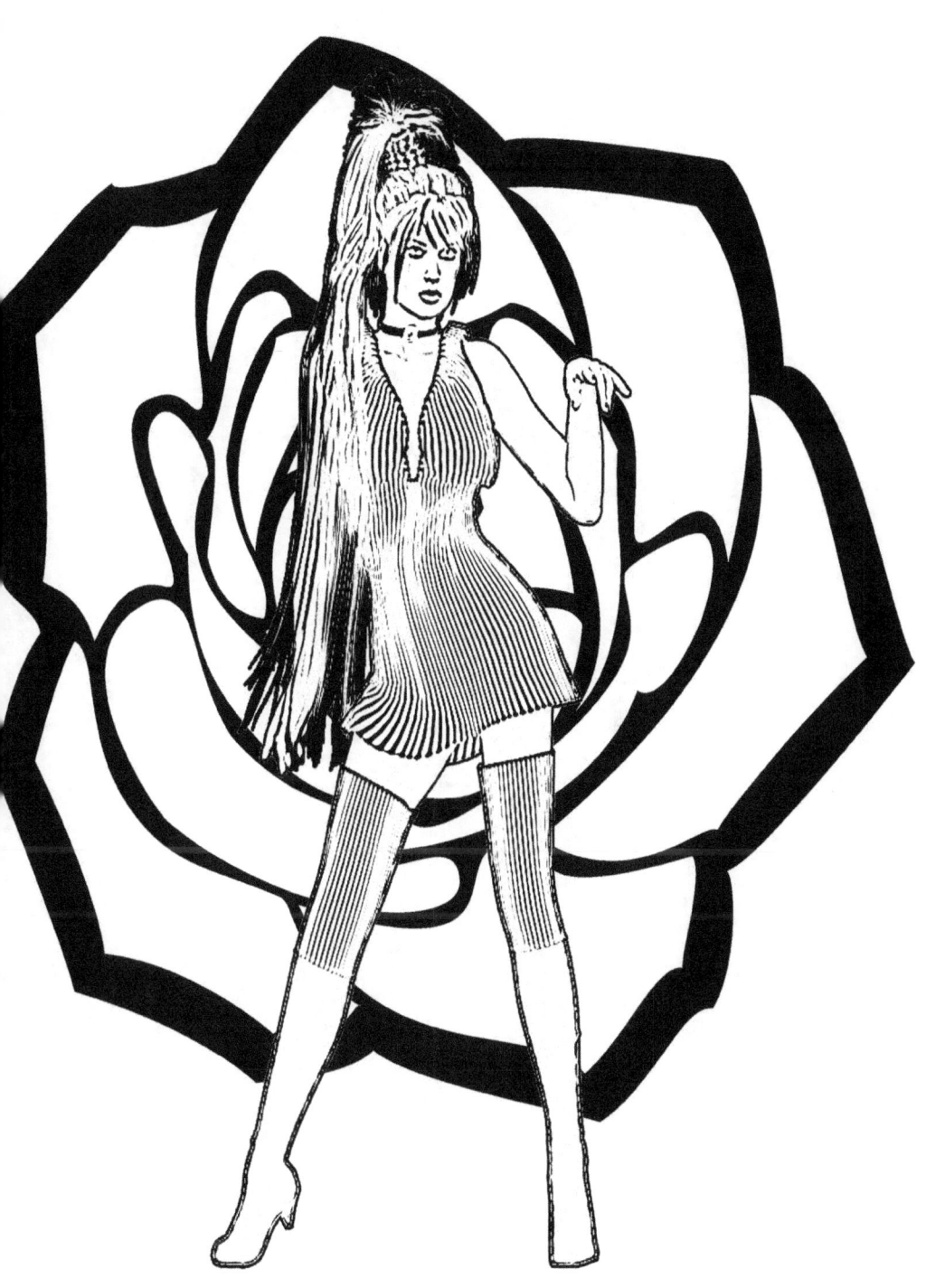

CTabaJones

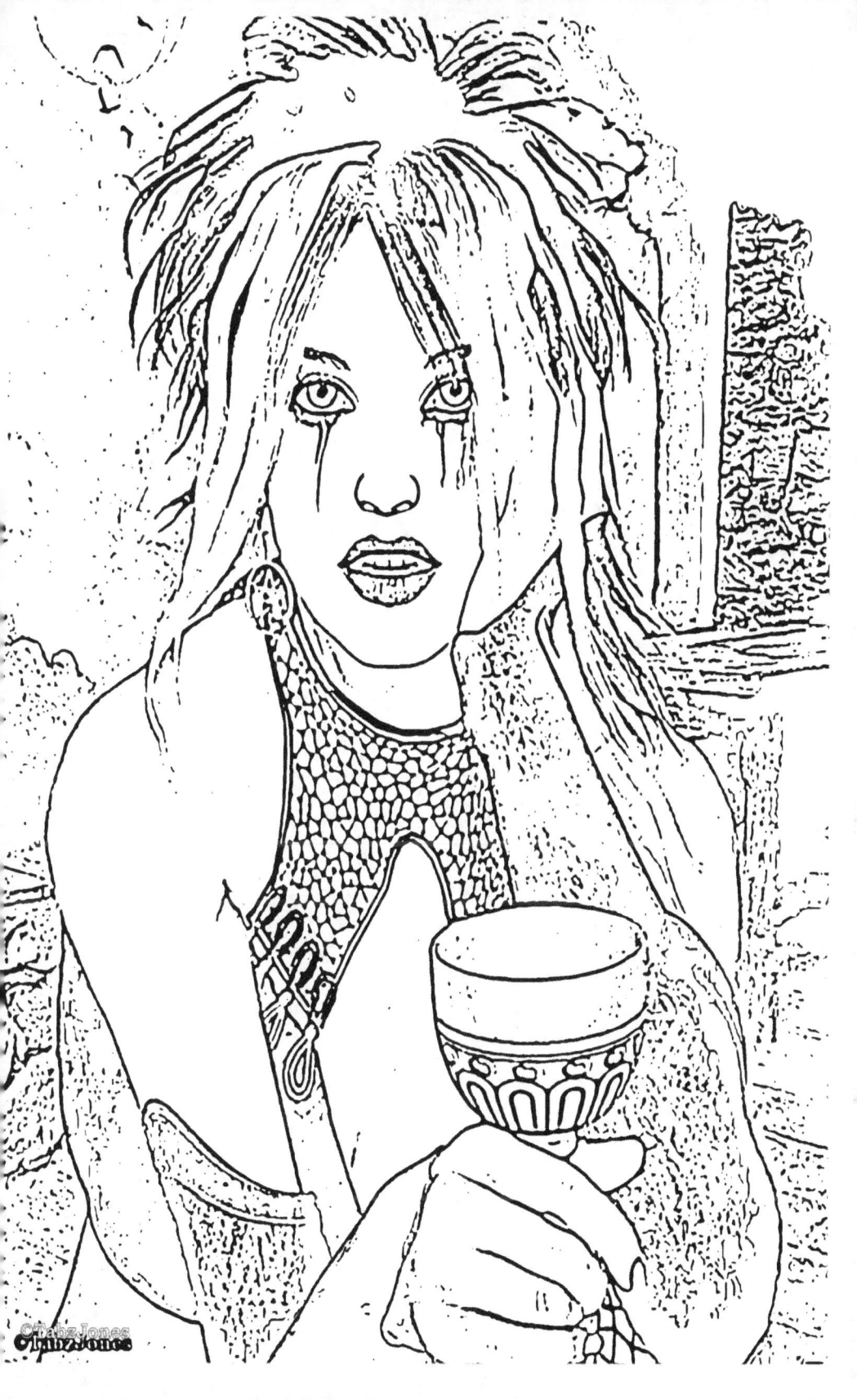

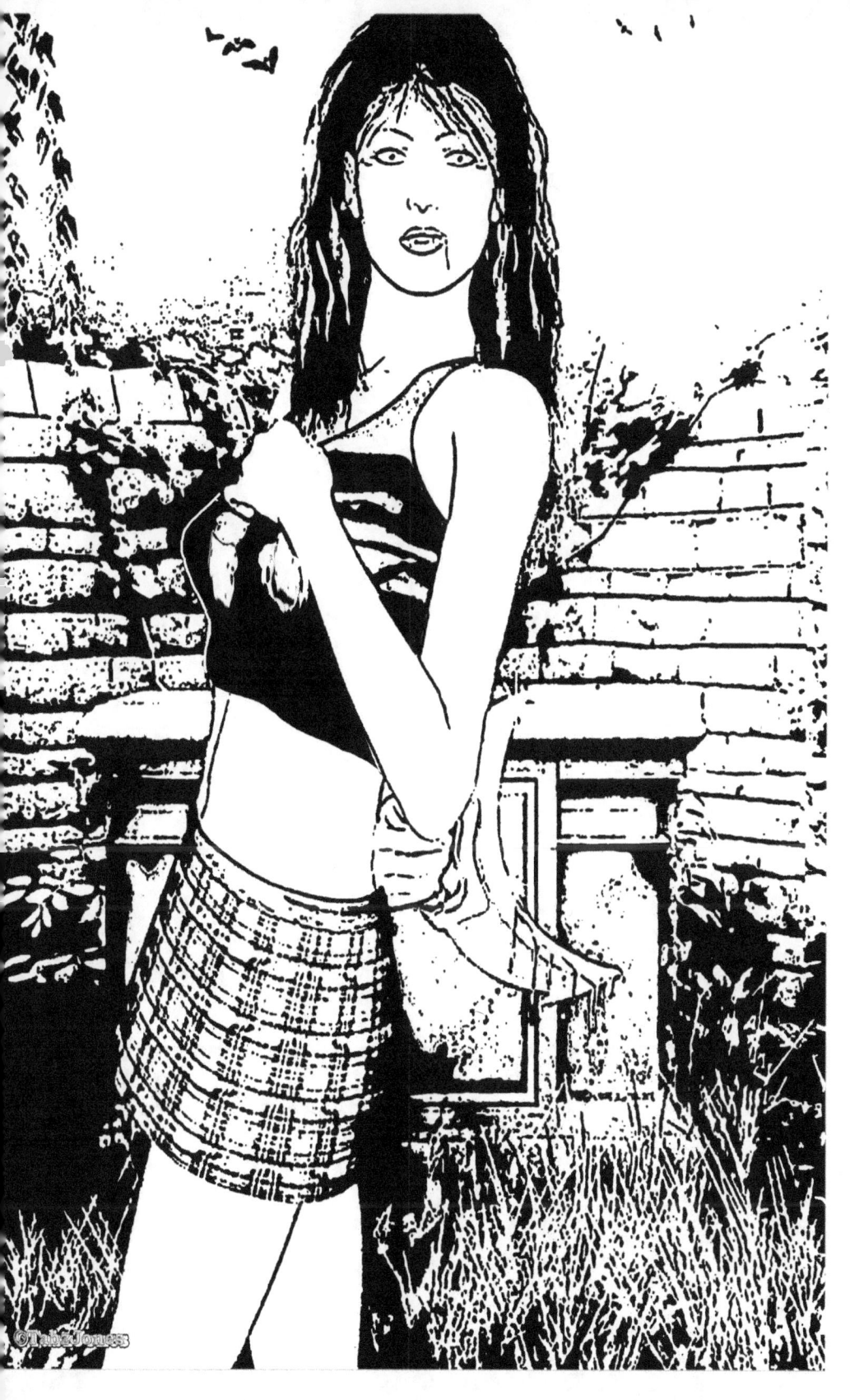

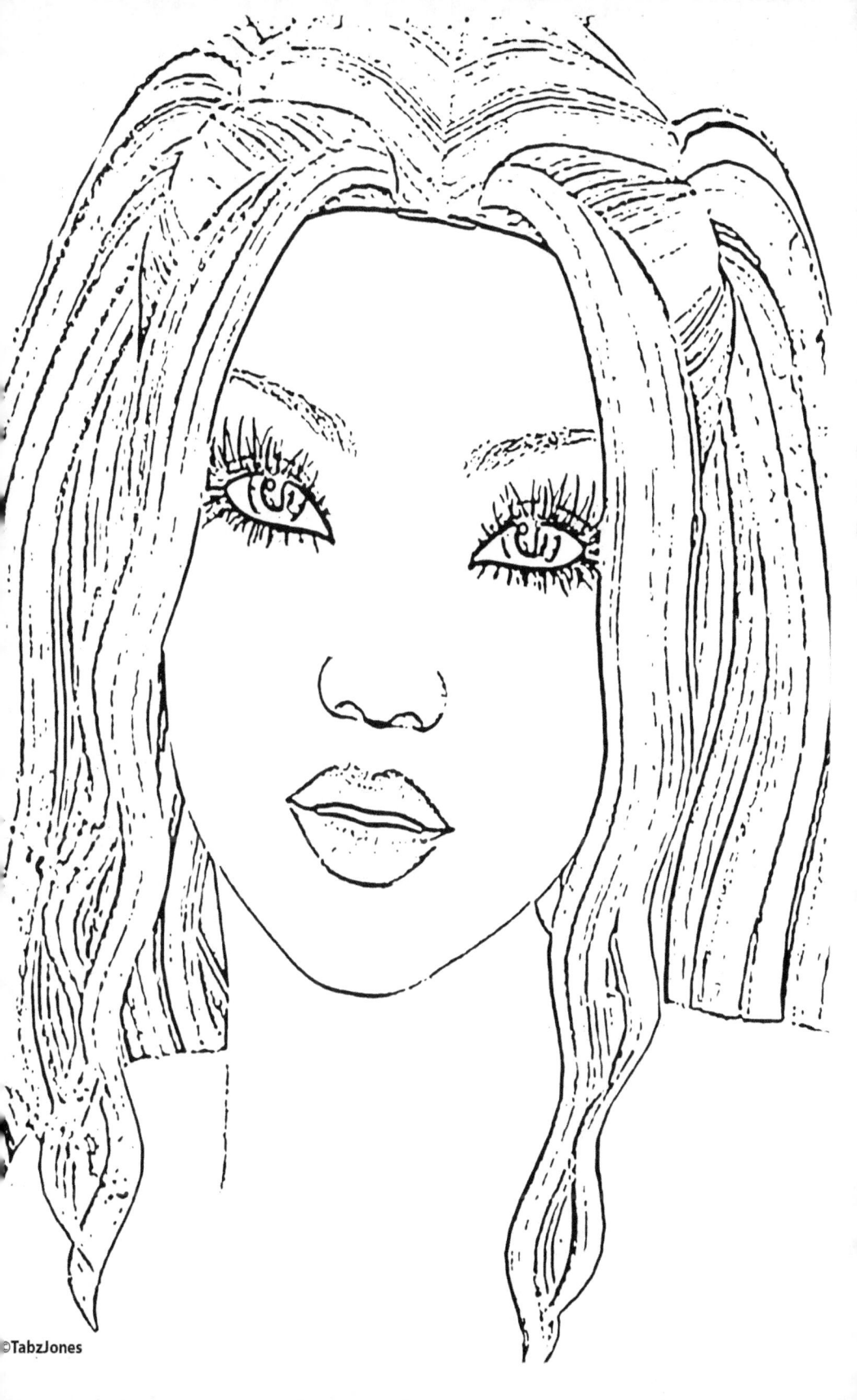

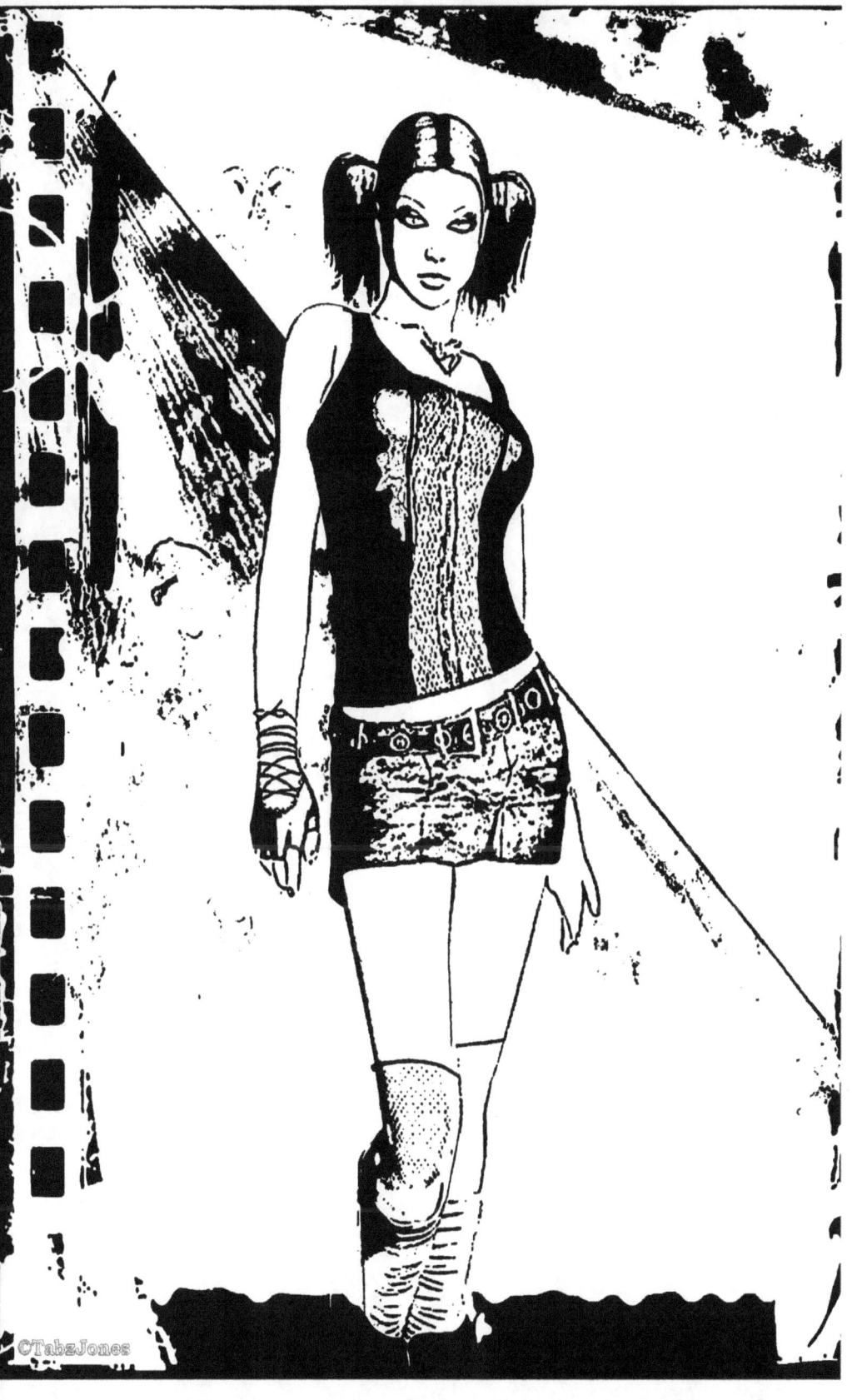

©TabzJones

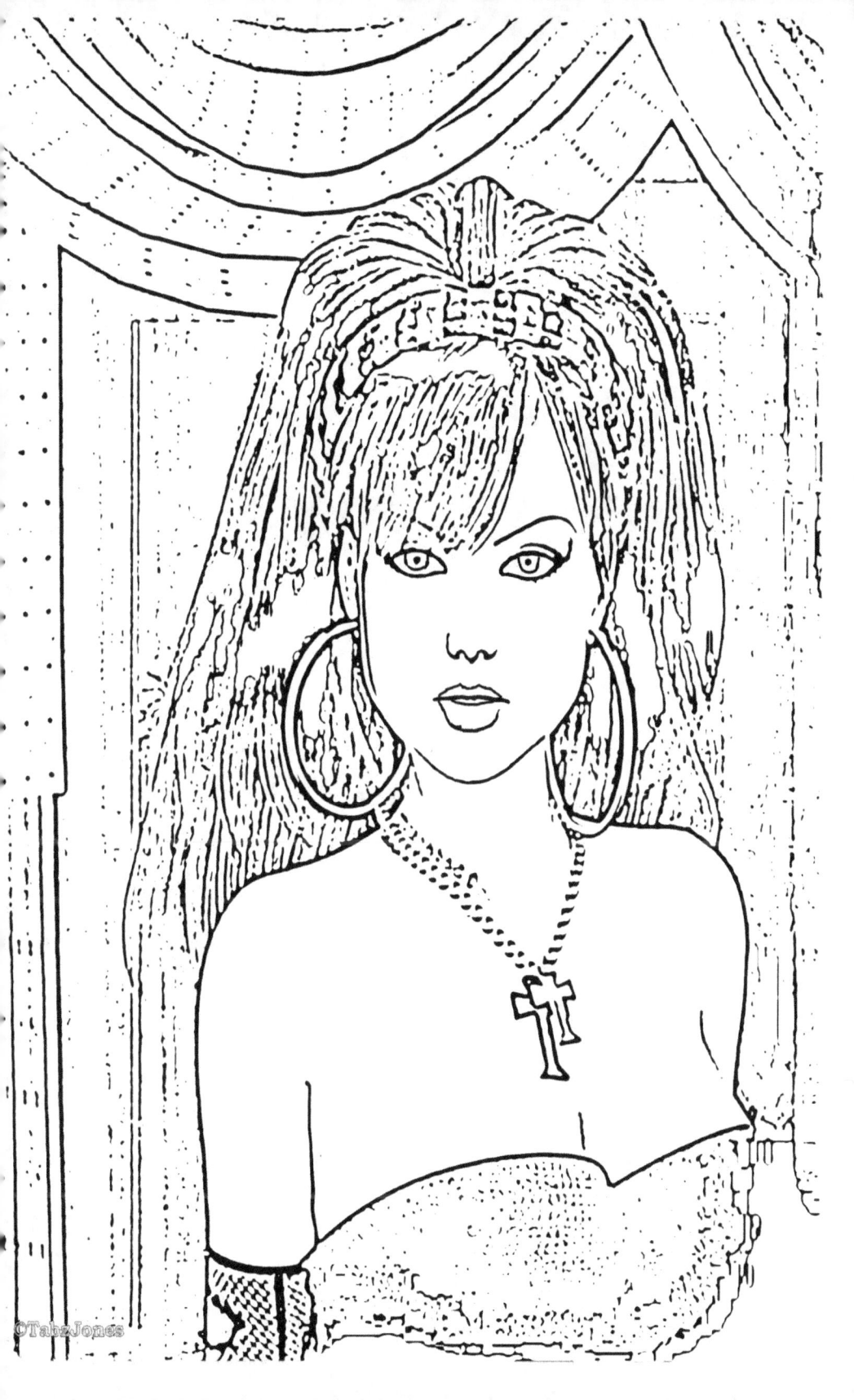
©TabzJones

www.ingramcontent.com/pod-product-compliance
Lightning Source LLC
Chambersburg PA
CBHW070402190526
45169CB00003B/1077